21st
Century
Junior
Library

WORKING AT A FACTORY

by Katie Marsico

CHERRY LAKE PUBLISHING * ANN ARBOR, MICHIGAN

CHERRY LAKE
Publishing

Published in the United States of America by Cherry Lake Publishing
Ann Arbor, Michigan
www.cherrylakepublishing.com

Content Adviser: Sharon Castle, PhD, Associate Professor of Elementary Social Studies,
George Mason University, Fairfax, VA

Reading Consultant: Cecilia Minden-Cupp, PhD, Literacy Specialist and Author

Photo Credits: Page 4, ©Jim West/Alamy; page 6, ©Julio Etchart/Alamy; page 8, ©JUPITERIMAGES/
Thinkstock/Alamy; cover and page 10, ©Baloncici, used under license from Shutterstock, Inc.; cover and
page 12, ©PhotoCreate, used under license from Shutterstock, Inc.; page 14, ©Bill Lyons/Alamy; page
16, ©vario images GmbH & Co.KG/Alamy; cover and page 18, ©PhotoCreate, used under license
from Shutterstock, Inc.; cover and page 20, ©Mauro Scarone, used under license from Shutterstock, Inc.

LIBRARY OF CONGRESS CATALOGING-IN-PUBLICATION DATA
Marsico, Katie, 1980–
Working at a factory / by Katie Marsico.
    p. cm.
Includes index.
ISBN-13: 978-1-60279-268-5
ISBN-10: 1-60279-268-2
1. Manufacturing industries—Vocational guidance—Juvenile literature.
2. Manufacturing industries—Employees—Juvenile literature.
3. Factories—Juvenile literature. I. Title.
HD9720.5.M385 2009

331.7'94—dc22   2008008541

Cherry Lake Publishing would like to acknowledge the work of
The Partnership for 21st Century Skills.
Please visit www.21stcenturyskills.org *for more information.*

CONTENTS

Many factory workers use machines
to make products.

What Is a Factory?

You hear whirring and buzzing sounds. People are working at machines. Where are you? You are visiting a **factory**!

A factory is where workers make items that are sold to stores. These items are called **products**. Factories make products you use every day.

Workers at this factory are making toy trucks.

Where do you think soap comes from? How about your favorite toys? These products were probably all made in factories.

Workers do many different jobs in factories. Let's take a look at some factory workers.

Look! Look around your home and your school. Can you name 10 products that were made in factories? Hint: chairs, books, and soup are a few examples.

A good foreperson is happy to help workers solve problems on the job.

Factory Workers

Many factory workers **operate** the machines that make the products. But there are other jobs, too.

Factory owners can't always be at the factory. So they depend on workers called **forepersons**. A foreperson is in charge of all the other workers. He answers their questions and shows them how to run the machines.

Some jobs in factories are done by robots!

There are usually several forepersons. Each one heads a different part of the factory. This is because workers do different jobs. Some operate machines. Others pack goods in boxes. The boxes are then shipped to stores.

Who creates these products? This is the job of **scientists** and **designers**. Scientists decide what should go into the products. Designers draw pictures that show how the product should look when it leaves the factory.

Some factory workers put products in cans.
Salespeople sell the cans to stores.

The factory owner also depends on **salespeople**. Salespeople sell the products the factory makes. They sell the products to stores where you can buy them.

Some factories make things that are used by other factories. Their salespeople sell those products to other factory owners.

Think!

Farmers grow vegetables. Who puts them in the cans you buy at the store? Hint: Think about who has machines that could be used to can the vegetables. Did you guess that factory workers put the vegetables in cans? You are correct!

Inspectors need to be able to take good notes
about problems they see in factories.

What other workers are important to a factory? **Inspectors** visit factories to make sure they are safe. They watch to see if workers are using the machines the right way. Inspectors also look at the machines themselves. A machine that is broken is often unsafe.

Do you see how a factory needs many workers to make the items you use every day? Each worker wants to give you the best possible product!

Don't be afraid to ask questions when touring a factory.

Do You Want to Work in a Factory?

Would you like a job in a factory someday? It is not too early to start thinking ahead! Ask your parents if they know of any factories that offer tours. Talk to workers if you visit a factory. Find out what skills they need to do their jobs.

Factory workers must be very careful when they use machines.

You might learn that many workers are good with machines. Most probably also pay close attention to rules. They care about safety.

Ask your parents to show you how different machines in your house work. Talk about which ones are safe for you to use if your parents show you how.

A factory can be an interesting place to work.

A factory can be an exciting place to work. Find out as much as you can now. This will help you decide if one of the jobs you have just read about is right for you!

Ask Questions!

Do you know someone who works in a factory? Talk to this worker. What does he like best about his work? What is the hardest part of working in a factory? Asking questions is a good way to learn about different jobs.

GLOSSARY

designers (di-ZYE-nerz) people who create plans that are used to make a product

factory (FAK-tree) a building where products are made

forepersons (FOR-per-sonz) people who are in charge of workers in different sections of the factory

inspectors (in-SPEK-tuhrz) people who make sure that factories are safe places for workers

operate (AH-peh-rayt) to handle or work a machine

products (PRAH-dukts) foods or other items that are sold in stores

salespeople (SAYLZ-pee-puhl) people who sell things or services

scientists (SYE-uhn-tists) people who study the world around us by testing and experimenting

FIND OUT MORE

BOOKS

The Engineering Is Elementary Team, and Jeannette Martin (illustrator). *Aisha Makes Work Easier: An Industrial Engineering Story*. Boston: Boston Museum of Science, 2005.

Pohl, Kathleen. *What Happens at a Toy Factory?* Milwaukee: Weekly Reader Early Learning Library, 2006.

WEB SITES

U.S. Department of Labor—Bureau of Labor Statistics (Science)
www.bls.gov/k12/science.htm
Click on "Chemist" and "Engineering Technician" to explore science jobs in factories

U.S. Department of Labor and U.S. Department of Education—Career Voyages: Advanced Manufacturing
www.careervoyages.gov/ advmanufacturing-videos.cfm
Watch videos about factory jobs

INDEX

ABOUT THE AUTHOR

Katie Marsico is the author of more than 30 children's books. She lives in Elmhurst, Illinois, with her husband and two children. She would especially like to thank her father-in-law, Frank Marsico (co-owner of the Mars Rubber factory), for helping her research this title.